A Course in

Self-Care - 2

Heal Your Body, Mind & Soul
Through Self-Love and Mindfulness

Ankita S.

This is book two in the *A Course in Self-Care* series. It is recommended that you complete book one before picking up this course.

Contents

Introduction

If you have read the first book, then you are already familiar with the 'introduction' and 'how to use this book' sections. I would still highly recommend that you re-read both of these chapters just as a revision. If you would much rather skip these, then feel free to start with the course straightaway.

Self-care is an act of self-love. It's a way of telling yourself that YOU matter – that your needs, wants and desires are important enough to be *joyously* met. The word 'joyously' is very important here as we often forget that taking care of our own self is truly a celebration of our existence.

In the true sense of the word, self-care isn't about just five or maybe twenty minutes of 'Me-time' every day. It's about creating a life in which you relish every moment of your existence. Real self-care is self-transformation in its highest form. It takes you to the realization that you are the creator of your own destiny and that you can have everything you want if only you allow yourself to believe so and work towards it.

Real self-care brings you in touch with who you truly are – your dreams, your hopes, your desires, and everything else that contributes to your definition of 'I' and mine. It helps you create a life of abundance and joy so that you never need a vacation from living that life.

This course will compel you to get in touch with your Truth. It might not be entirely comfortable at first but I urge you to persist no matter what. An amazing life isn't built by living within one's comfort zone.

I want you to push yourself to your limits and fall completely in love with yourself every day from now onwards. Creating the life of your dreams is the highest form of self-care. Of course, the exclusive 'Me-time' every day is the cherry on the cake that makes the process even more delightful.

Every human being is a complex organism physiologically, psychologically and emotionally. At the spiritual level, we are all made of the same fabric but the way our identities manifest in the material world is always unique. The problem with society is that it epitomizes one way of being as the only ideal everyone must aspire for.

For instance, at one point of time in history, women with rounded figures were held as the ultimate paragons of beauty. In our present times, being reed thin has become the norm and everyone is aspiring to look like an emaciated runway model.

Hence, in our society, it's considered radical when someone is brave enough to just be himself or herself. From now onwards, I want you to focus on who you really are. Instead of taking everything for granted and believing that you are this way or that way, I want you to get in the habit of questioning everything.

Surely, this is not going to be comfortable at first but you must get comfortable with being uncomfortable. After all, we come face-to-face with our real potential only after stepping outside the comfort zone.

I want you to find your own definition of success and become very successful. Just remember that real success is what happens within you and not necessarily outside of you. Who you become in the process of acquiring everything you have aspired for is far more important than the material wealth you have managed to amass.

I want to also remind you that health is the greatest wealth and peace of mind is the most precious asset (the only one worth guarding with all your might and at all costs). Success doesn't necessarily mean doing more – it means being at peace with who you are, where you have come from and where you are going. Real freedom doesn't come from having more but from wanting less. You don't become rich by hoarding more objects and money but from how richly you live your life while using with gratitude that which you do own. Being rich is about being content and real contentment doesn't come from wanting more but from giving more.

What Self-Care is Not?

We live in a strange world. While it's considered perfectly 'natural' to complain about life and walk around looking like a martyr, it's usually not seen in good light when a person proclaims that he loves himself or herself. Such a person is immediately termed a narcissist and made to feel guilty about how he or she feels.

In my opinion, the glorified self-effacement that is done in the name of humility is far more dangerous as it not only damages our self-esteem but also leaves us seeking approval and acknowledgement from others.

Narcissism versus Self-Love

There is a clear distinction between narcissism and self-love. A narcissist is someone who is obsessed with himself to the point that he thinks he is superior to anyone else. He doesn't mind going to any extent to prove this fallacy as truth.

On the other hand, someone with a tremendous amount of self-love possesses a very healthy sense of Self. She loves and accepts herself unconditionally without making comparisons with others. She is well aware of her flaws and is constantly working to be the best version of herself without any sense of self-loathing or guilt.

Hence, the primary difference between a narcissist and a self-loving person is the motivation they are driven by. The narcissist lives from a place of fear and ego because he has to constantly strive to look and appear better than everyone else. He cares a great deal about how others perceive him as he must command the adulation of others. A self-loving person, on the other hand, lives from a place of unconditional love and non-judgmental acceptance. She is not influenced by how other people see her as her sense of self is inherently very strong. There is nothing to prove to anyone or any unnecessary interest in how other people perceive her.

While it might look like the narcissist has a lot of self-confidence that is generally not the case. What he is showing to the world is usually just a facade of false ego. Anyone who is guided purely by love will never compare himself with another person. The narcissist is rather too preoccupied with proving how he compares and fares better in comparison with others.

Self-love, on the other hand, is guided by self-reliance. You learn to rely on yourself for meeting your need for approval, acceptance and appreciation. Hence, self-love goes hand-in-hand with self-acceptance. You have to accept yourself unconditionally in order to have real self-love.

It's important to remember that your relationship with yourself is the most important relationship for you in the whole world. Every other relationship is merely a reflection of this one relationship. Believe it or not, this is the truth. If you delve deep into this relationship, you will develop the insight to understand every other relationship in your life.

For example, if you feel that others don't accept you for who you are, then, you must analyze if you fully accept your own self unconditionally and without judgment. If you feel that others are critical of you, then, you must do some soul-searching to find out how critical you are of yourself.

People will always perceive you the way you perceive your own self, and I am not talking about what you believe to be true at the conscious level. Your behavior and your reactions are shaped by the impressions registered in the subconscious mind.

Self-Care Begins with Self-Acceptance

Self-care begins with self-acceptance. Just like you cannot love someone else unconditionally without first accepting them completely and without judgment, the same is true for you.

If the aircraft was about to crash, you will put on your own oxygen mask first, and only then help others, you must always look after yourself first. By taking good care of yourself, you build the ability to derive strength, nourishment, and sustenance from your own soul. You don't need another person to make you feel better about yourself because you are already feeling amazing.

This way you are able to have deeper and more meaningful relationships with others as you no longer enter relationships from a place of need. All your relationships become based on the desire to give unconditionally and wholeheartedly. When the other person does something good for you, you feel ecstatic because you were not expecting anything. Letting go of all expectations is the best thing you can do to experience great joy and gratitude in your relationships.

It's not too far-fetched to say that taking excellent care of yourself and loving yourself unconditionally is the pre-requisite for having deep meaningful relationships with others.

Never forget that you cannot pour from an empty cup.

What Self-Care is Not

So let's first dismiss all the wrong ideas people have about self-care.

SELF-CARE IS NOT:

- Selfishness
- Self-absorption
- Narcissism
- Egotism
- Egocentrism
- Ostentation
- Superiority complex
- Being Vainglorious

Now, the question is what to do if someone else tells you that you are any of the above just because you love yourself and like taking care of yourself?

The answer lies in understanding other people. You must ascertain the fact that most people don't like themselves, and they find it very hard to understand how anyone else can be so happy with their own self.

There is also a lot of guilt and shame associated with feeling good about oneself. These negative emotions are so deeply imprinted in people's psyche that they try to put down anyone who manages to break out of this cycle of shame of guilt. This doesn't mean that they are bad people who are consciously trying to put others down. They are most likely doing this unconsciously (at least, in most cases) behind the smokescreen of good intentions. Most people are too badly trapped by the mental conditioning they have received from family, society and educational institutions. They find it difficult to understand that they are encaged in a dangerous cycle of self-loathing that often manifests as loathing towards others.

The right way to deal with someone like this is to treat them with empathy and compassion. For this, you have to be mindful of where they are coming from. A person who loves himself will never try to bring another person down. We don't see others the way they are, but we see a reflection of our own self in others.

Understand that whatever they are saying about you has nothing to do with you – it has everything to do with how they see their own self.

What is Self-Care?

As stated earlier self-care begins with self-acceptance. You must know who you truly are and accept yourself unconditionally. In fact, I don't even like to use the word 'accept' in this context. The right term would be 'embrace yourself unconditionally.' There are already enough critics in the world to bring people down. Why join their league and become your own worst enemy?

Where there is acceptance, love always follows. Love can never exist without acceptance preceding it first. In this book, you will take this journey with me from self-acceptance to self-love. Self-care comes automatically in the presence of these two.

If you do each assignment exactly as instructed, then, you certainly will succeed in creating a happier life for yourself. Self-care is so incredibly empowering that you will be amazed by all the transformations that will occur in your life.

Self-care is greatly emancipating because it makes you lose the desire or need to seek approval from others. You no longer get easily hurt by other people's words and actions. And even if you do feel hurt, you are able to respond back with calmness and composure.

Put Yourself First

Caring for yourself means taking out time for yourself every single day. It means understanding your needs and putting yourself first. After all, if you are second priority to your own self, then, everyone else in your life will also treat you that way.

SELF-CARE IS:

✓ Knowing the needs of your body, mind and soul
✓ Fulfilling your needs with joy and gratitude
✓ Honoring your desires and wants
✓ Taking out time for yourself without feeling guilty
✓ Exercising regularly and eating healthy
✓ Feeding positive ideas and thoughts into your mind

✓ Spending money on yourself without guilt

✓ Getting comfortable receiving compliments graciously and without undue self-effacement

✓ Saying a clear 'NO' to people, situations and places that suck your energy

✓ Spending time with those you love and/or who make you feel good about yourself

✓ Guarding yourself against negativity

✓ Not letting criticism or the negative words/opinions of others affect you

✓ Practicing compassion and forgiveness towards your own self (this will automatically make it easier for you to forgive others)

✓ Looking in the mirror and admiring everything you love about yourself

✓ Being grateful for everything you have and the person that you are

✓ Being kind to your body by listening to what it's telling you

✓ Constantly engaging in positive self-talk and encouragement

✓ Getting up and making a stronger comeback every single time you fall down

✓ Believing that you are the most important person in your world and treating yourself that way

✓ Doing whatever it takes to retain your happiness and positivity each day

The 10 Commandments of Self-Care

I recommend that you read these 10 commandments every day. You can paste them on your wall so that you are constantly reminded to practice them.

1. Love and accept yourself (unconditionally) first. Loving and accepting everyone else will come easily after this.
2. Take care of your body. This body is the only real home you have for living in this world.
3. Think positive, speak positive and listen only to what's positive.
4. Rely only on your own self. Believe that YOU have the power to make all your dreams come true. Do not seek approval from anyone else – believe in your own self no matter what anyone else says. If something feels right, then just trust your heart and go for it.
5. Make compliments a way of life. Give them generously to yourself and to others. If someone gives you a compliment, accept them graciously.
6. Treat yourself with dignity and respect. Walk away from everything that no longer serves your Highest Good.
7. Make your entire life a labor of love. Dream and create a life you don't need any days off from.
8. Every day, take the time to connect with Nature in some way. She is your mother entering her womb will take you closer to your own Truth
9. Compete only with your own self. Strive to constantly be a better than the best version of yourself.

10. Be completely honest with yourself – take responsibility for your life and for everything that you are experiencing right now.

Always Listen to Your Heart

I'll end this chapter with a little advice that you'd want to remember all throughout this course and also for the rest of your life. You'd want to hold on really tight to this piece of wisdom.

If you really want something, just go for it! Don't let anyone tell you it's not possible, it cannot be done, it's not practical. Life is what you make of it. Everything is a creation and if you are relying on someone else's idea of what's possible and what's not, then you are imposing their self-created limitations on your own life. Don't listen to anyone who says it can't be done. Learn to be your own best friends. Believe in your dreams and go after what you want.

How to Use This Book

This book is designed as a course meant to be taken over a period of three months.

This is the second book in the *A Course in Self-Care* series. If you haven't completed the first course, then I would advise that you start with book one. Come back to this book once you have completed the three month course that's laid out in book one.

There are four lessons in each month that are meant to be studied and practiced every day of the week. If you want you can read the entire book in one go but to get maximum benefits out of this carefully designed course, I'd suggest taking things slow and following the step-by-step instructions.

You'll experience great transformation if you do all the exercises that are suggested for the week. I'll suggest starting out on a Sunday or a Monday so that it is easier for you to keep track of your progress. This isn't imperative – you can start on any day of the week – all you have to do is keep track of your progress properly.

It's very important that you are doing something for yourself every single day over a period of three months as you are establishing a habit here. At first, it might be very difficult for you to find time for yourself.

When you do something with consistency for a period of 21 days, it starts becoming a habit. Over time, self-care will become such a natural part of your routine that it will become as pivotal as brushing your teeth and taking a shower every day.

What if You Miss a Day?

In a perfect world, you will be reading and practicing the weekly lesson every day. However, things happen. Sometimes life just gets in the way and we feel like we have little control over our day.

My advice would be to avoid a situation like this as much as possible. Discipline is a pre-requisite for success in any area of life. If despite your best efforts, you end up missing a day, then, I would say get back to the schedule as soon as you can.

What you must watch out for is the trap of "I'll start tomorrow." This usually happens if you miss one day. Then, you will feel so guilty about having missed a day that you'd find it difficult to regain the momentum. This is the real danger with missing one day. It makes you lose your momentum and leaves you with guilt.

If you miss a day, then just accept it lovingly and try your best to not let it happen again. Don't beat yourself about it and don't allow yourself to feel guilty under any circumstance. Start from where you had left and you'd do great.

However, you must guard against making a habit out of this. Self-care is an empowering habit that you are building, and every day that you spend doing something good for yourself counts in helping you internalize it more deeply.

What if You Want to Skip a Lesson or an Activity

I would highly recommend that you practice every single lesson outlined in this course. A lot of times the mind will try talking us out of something that is difficult for us. You have to understand that this perception of difficulty usually stems from deep-seated mental blocks. If you practice each lesson for the entire week, then you will surely experience a shift – it might be a small or a big one but the shift will surely happen.

You might want to skip some activities – I would recommend that you try doing each activity at least for a few days if not for the entire week. This will help you understand whether it's something you can incorporate into your daily routine for the long-term or not. Ideally, practice each activity for at least a week.

Some activities will be especially enjoyable to you and those are the ones you'd want to adopt for life or for as long you wish to be practicing them.

How to Get the Most Out of This Book

➤ Read the weekly lesson every day of the week. Ideally, read it twice a day – right after waking up and immediately before going to bed.

➤ Maintain a daily journal in which you set goals for each day based on the instructions for the week.

➤ Feel free to take notes and make highlights in the book wherever necessary.

➤ Keep this book as a companion with you at all times. Some of you might find it helpful to own both a digital and paperback version of this book so that you can make highlights and take notes in the paperback version and use the digital version for a quick read throughout the day.

➤ Even though each lesson is meant to be studied for one week, you don't have to become perfect at it within such a timeframe. What's important is to make your best effort throughout the week and then continue the learning process for as long as it takes. You can progress to the next week's lesson while also continuing to master the previous week's lesson.

➤ For convenience, it might be better to read the first lesson of this book on a Sunday and start implementing it from Monday. This way, you'd know what to expect to be doing in the first week of the course. Starting on a Monday and ending the week on a Sunday will also help you in keeping track of your weekly progress.

➤ As you progress from week to week and lesson to lesson, you'd want to naturalize everything you are learning into a routine. Be sure to include those activities that you enjoy most in your daily or weekly routine.

➤ This is the kind of book that you'd want to keep coming back to time and again. The more number of times you go through the course, the greater will be your mastery over it. I recommend that once you finish the course, you restart it from lesson 1. Alternatively, you can choose to go through those lessons that you found especially enjoyable or those that were a challenge for you and where you feel you need to make considerable progress.

➤ If you have someone in your life who is on the same wavelength as you and that person would be interested in something like this, then, I would highly recommend doing the course with that person. Having an accountability buddy will help you make greater progress as you both will keep a check on each other's progress.

These are only some of the recommendations that I feel will be helpful to anyone who wants to get the most out of this book. However, you must experiment and see what works for you and what does not. Use your creative freedom to find your own way of getting the most out of this course.

To make a start somewhere, use the guidelines stated above. If something seems to work, then stick with it. If it doesn't, then find what works best for you and stay with it.

The

Self-Care Course - 2

Week 1 – Self-Forgiveness

Forgiveness is something that most people struggle with. We find it hard to forgive others for the wrongs they might have done to us. It is even harder to forgive ourselves for the wrongs we think we have done to others.

The interesting thing is that once we start practicing forgiveness towards our own self, it gets easier to forgive others as well.

Forgiveness and gratitude are the two pillars of a happy life. If you want to be happy in life, then radical forgiveness is the only way to get there. You must constantly forgive yourself and others.

We will discuss gratitude in more depth in another chapter. It will be our theme for week 3. For now, let us focus on forgiveness.

Why is it important to forgive yourself?

We are often extremely hard on ourselves. We beat ourselves up for two reasons: the things that we did wrong and the things that we think we did wrong.

The difference between the two is that sometimes our actions have indeed caused some kind of harm to another person. In the second scenario, we think that our actions have harmed the other person but that might not actually be the case or how that other person perceives it.

My suggestion to you is that every time you feel you have done something wrong; take an objective look at the situation. Ask yourself why you behaved the way you did. Was that the best you knew at that time and place or maybe you lost control in that moment acting in a way that's not typical of you?

Be Kind to Yourself

Have empathy for yourself. This isn't the same as making excuses for yourself. What has been done has already happened. You can't change it but you can learn from the experience and become a better person.

Instead of harboring guilt, you can embrace the lesson and become a better person. Guilt is a worthless emotion anyway. Nothing good has ever come out of feeling guilty. It keeps you stuck in the past and makes you feel powerless.

Your power lies in transforming the feeling of guilt into something positive. Just decide that from this moment forward, you will be a different person.

Shift the Energy

Also, it's true that on one level, the past can never be changed. But this isn't the truth at the spiritual level. The past, present, and future exist within this moment. By shifting your energy in the present moment, you are positively influencing both the past and the future.

Every time you feel, you have done something wrong, pause for a moment and ask yourself, how would you do it differently now?

Ask for Forgiveness

Don't shy away from asking for forgiveness from others. Very few people have the ability to take ownership for their actions and behavior.

Sometimes a negative situation can be transmuted into a positive one by simply taking responsibility. You will also feel like a huge weight has been removed from your chest once you admit your fault and seek forgiveness. It won't make you small in any way. Only a big person can bend down and seek forgiveness.

A lot of times we also do wrong to our own self. Don't hesitate from asking your own self to forgive you as well. You just didn't know any better when it happened but now you have become a better person who is capable and determined enough to take good care of himself or herself.

Tasks for This Week:

The Forgiveness List

➤ Write down all the wrongs that you have done to your own self (example, abusing your body with alcohol, fast food, calling yourself names like 'fat' 'useless' 'good for nothing' etc.)

➤ Create a list of all the wrongs you have done to others that you still beat yourself about. It doesn't matter how long ago it happened. If it's gnawing on your conscience, then it is something worth noting down.

Forgiving Yourself

➤ Write an apology letter to yourself. Address it to yourself, like "my dear Self" or your name or whatever feels right to your heart. Write down how deeply sorry you are for all the ways in which you have wronged yourself. If you feel like crying, allow the tears to flow. Once you have written down how sorry you are about doing something wrong, follow it up with what you are going to do to make amends for it.

For example, "I am really sorry that I have fed you bad food for so many years. Please forgive me as at that time I didn't have the knowledge, understanding, and wisdom that I have now. From now onwards, I will feed you high-quality wholesome food."

➤ It might take you a while to write down an apology for every single wrongdoing. However, continue with this even if it takes you longer than a week. After a while, it won't be as overwhelming as it would be initially when you get started. You can start doing the actions and exercises of week 2 as well once the first week is over.

➤ When you're ready, burn the letter. But before burning the letter, be sure to write down on another piece of paper all the things that your improved self will be doing as promised in that letter. Read that list every day to make sure that you are staying on track and keeping your promises to yourself. After burning the letter, it is a good idea to immerse the ashes in a moving water body (like the river or sea). If that's not doable, then even your toilet flush would do.

➤ Once you have completed everything that was on your list, I want you to turn this into a way of life. Every day, reflect on the wrongs that you might have done to yourself (if any), and then, write down a few lines seeking forgiveness from yourself and promising to be better moving forward.

<u>Seeking Forgiveness from Others</u>

➤ If you are like most people, you probably have quite a long list of things that you think you have done wrong to others.

➤ For this week, I want you to pick out 3 people to whom you feel you have done the greatest wrongs. Write an apology letter to them listing every single thing that you feel you have done wrong. Just like you did in the letter to yourself, write down how you are committed to being a better person moving forward (be sure that it's something that you genuinely feel you want to and can do).

➤ You have two choices here; you can either hand over that apology to the person you have wronged or you can burn that letter. What you might choose to do in this situation would differ based on the type of relationship you have with that person and if that person is around or not. Do what feels right to your heart. Either way, you will feel a huge shift in energy once you complete this task. In case you are burning the letter, it is a good idea to immerse the ashes in a moving water body (like the river or sea). If that's not doable, then go with the toilet flush.

➤ Once you are done apologizing to the three people, gradually work your way through the rest of the list. Once you have completed the list, make it a way of life to apologize to people immediately after you feel you have done something wrong. This will keep your conscience clean and you will also enjoy better relationships with others. It takes a lot of courage and strength to take ownership of one's mistakes. Most people will admire you for it, and, more often than not, you will receive the forgiveness that you are seeking.

Week 2 – Forgiving Others

When we hold a grudge against someone or believe that they are the cause of our misery, we are actually giving them power over our own self. We are saying that they have the ability to make us feel happy or sad.

Why would you want to give that kind of power to anyone else?

What Does it Mean to Forgive Someone?

Most people also think that forgiving someone means condoning their actions. Let me clarify properly what I mean by forgiveness.

When you harbor anger or resentment towards someone, you are basically keeping yourself imprisoned inside a dark room of negativity. Anger affects your health negatively. As Buddha said, "Holding onto anger is like drinking poison and expecting the other person to die."

You can't go back in time and change what has already happened. But what you can do is transform the memory of that experience into something positive. Everything happens for a reason. Within every challenging experience, there is always a lesson that our soul has chosen to learn in this lifetime.

Embrace the lesson – let go of the resentment and anger. At the spiritual level, the souls who seem to cause us a lot of trouble in this life are actually serving us. They are helping us evolve spiritually.

I even read somewhere that it is the souls that love us the most who take on the hardest roles to play out in this life so that we can get the experiences we need to evolve spiritually.

True Forgiveness is Freeing

By forgiving the other person, we are freeing them and ourselves from a prison that we have created inside our minds. Hence, your goal should be to shift your perception from one of wrongdoing to that of embracing the lesson.

Challenging life circumstances are there to help us become stronger and better. Just like you get physically stronger by lifting heavy weights in the gym, you get stronger by overcoming challenging life circumstances.

The Purpose of Life

At the soul level, every person has chosen to go through certain experiences in this lifetime. Once we arrived here, we forgot what we came here for. Life is not meant to be easy, it is meant to be evolutionary so that our soul can attain its highest potential.

Besides, how is your unforgiveness serving you? Can anything good ever come out of it? All it does is take away from you the potential of being fully happy in the present moment. Let go of the past – it is nothing but an illusion.

Making Peace with the Past

I must share with you a beautiful quote that I read somewhere:

"Forgiveness is giving up the hope that the past could have been any different, it's accepting the past for what it was, and using this moment and this time to help yourself move forward." – Oprah Winfrey

Forgiveness is indeed an acceptance of the past for what it was. When we are no longer struggling in the here and now to change something that happened long ago, we find peace.

Forgive others not because they deserve it, but because you deserve to move forward and live in peace. You don't even need to verbally tell someone you have forgiven them. If you think it is a good idea to tell them so, then by all means go ahead and convey your message. But it's not mandatory.

Real forgiveness brings about a shift in energy that immediately changes our reality. It is up to you to turn your past negative experience into something beautiful by embracing the lesson that was gifted to you through that challenge.

Here's another beautiful quote that might inspire you to become a more forgiving person.

"Forgiveness is the fragrance that the violet sheds on the heel that has crushed it."

– Mark Twain.

Make forgiveness a way of life. Let go of all grudges. Don't keep any memory of wrongdoings. Yes, do make note of your less than pleasant experiences so that you can be cautious next time. But for your own sake, don't hold onto any form of negativity. It will only create blockages in your life.

Don't Form Negative Entanglements

We often get very strongly attached to the people we hold a grudge against. Even if we aren't physically around them often, they become part of our energy field. Why would you want that?

Let them go. Keep your focus on your own growth and evolution. That will truly serve you in the long-run.

Also, it is important to realize that most people are doing their best based on their level of understanding and personal evolution. You might not like their words, behavior, or actions but have empathy for the fact that they didn't know any better when they wronged you.

In their mind, they might not know or understand that their words or behavior could harm you. If it's someone close to you, you can help them understand how you feel without putting any blame on them (non-violent communication).

Like for instance, instead of saying, "You have hurt me so much," you can say, "I felt deeply hurt by the words …. It made me feel …" This would disarm them a bit as you are making yourself vulnerable without putting the blame on them.

A lot of problems in life can be solved through clear communication. Learning to communicate non-violently is the greatest skill you can acquire in life.

Tasks for This Week:

➤ Write down the name of every person who has ever wronged you.

➤ Pick 3 people who you feel have wronged you the most. Write a letter to them sharing how you feel. Again, steer clear of blame. Focus on sharing how you feel and the ways in which their words/actions have affected you.

➤ When you are ready, either give the letter to the person it is addressed to or you can burn it just like how you did in week 1. Avoid getting upset if you don't get a response (that you like) from the other person.

➤ Do this for every person who you think has wronged you. Take your time and have patience with yourself and others.

➤ Again, turn this into a way of life. Don't allow resentment to form when you feel someone has wronged you. Instead, focus on sharing how you feel by learning to communicate non-violently. I would highly recommend that you read *Nonviolent Communication: A Language of Life* by Marshall B. Rosenberg.

Week 3 – The Magic of Gratitude

I started by naming this chapter 'gratitude' but then decided to make it 'the magic of gratitude' because gratitude is truly magical. We started some gratitude practices in book one but, in this course, we are going to go much deeper into the practice of gratitude.

The secret to a happy life lies in mastering the basics – gratitude is one of them.

Practicing gratitude in your daily life is the best gift you can give to yourself. Your daily experiences will shift completely once gratitude becomes a way of life for you.

Count Your Blessings

Gratitude is all about counting your blessings every day and every moment of life. It's about seeing the glass half-full no matter what's actually happening in your life. Nothing is inherently good or bad. It's your perception that creates your reality.

For instance, I remember watching this documentary called *Happy*. The narrator interviewed people from different walks of life to ask whether they were happy or not.

There was a man who lived in the slums of India. He had very few material comforts and even had a leaky roof above his head. Yet he was very happy and had a lot of good things to say about his life.

One can live in a palace surrounded by luxuries and still be miserable. I am not saying that you shouldn't aspire to live a materially comfortable life. But the point is that it is all about attitude.

Having an attitude of gratitude is more important than owning luxuries and material comforts.

Practicing Gratitude Multiplies Your Blessings

While we won't be covering Law of Attraction in this book, I want you to understand one basic law of the Universe. Whatever you think about the most is what you get to experience in your material reality.

If you are constantly thinking about everything that's not right in your life, you are attracting more of it into your reality. On the other hand, by focusing on being grateful for all your blessings, you will be attracting more good things into your life.

I hope you have continued with the practice of writing 3 things you are grateful for every morning and evening (from book one). If not, get back to the habit of doing it. This is a practice you want to retain for life. It will play a phenomenal role in helping you live a happy and fulfilling life.

From now on, I would also like you to get into the habit of saying 'thank you.' Every time someone does something for you – big or small – say a heartfelt thank you to them. Don't ever take anyone or anything for granted.

Every time, you do something good for yourself, thank yourself for it too. You are also a person who deserves appreciation and gratitude.

Tasks for This Week:

➤ Every morning, write down 2 things you are grateful for. Every night, before going to bed, write down 3 things that happened in your day that you are grateful for. Challenge yourself to come up with something new every day.

➤ This week, be sure to say thank you to anyone who does something for you – big or small. Be generous with your compliments and stingy with your criticisms.

➤ Express gratitude to yourself every time you are doing something good for yourself. Like, when you manage to take yourself to the gym or stick to a balanced diet.

➤ Express gratitude towards the things you own and the surroundings you live in by taking care of them. Cleaning and maintaining them are also forms of gratitude. Treat your possessions and your living space with reverence and gratitude.

Week 4 – Make the Everyday More Pleasurable & Beautiful

We have discussed some of these ideas in book one but now it is time to go even deeper into making your everyday life more pleasurable and beautiful.

This is one of the most important things you have to master. Hence, it is worth discussing some of the practices I encouraged you to adopt in book one along with a few added tips and a more in-depth discussion around this subject.

Are You Living Your Best Life Daily?

How do you prepare for a special day? Do you pull out your best clothes, make an effort to look your best, and be your best?

How do you feel on such days? Don't you feel completely over the moon?

My question is why aren't you doing this every day then?

It seems like as a society we have our priorities backward. We make an effort to look our best in public while we allow ourselves to be our frumpiest worst when it's just us and our loved ones around.

Shouldn't we be our best on a daily basis for our own self and for the people we love most?

Live Every Day as if it Were Your Last

How would you live if tomorrow was meant to be your last day in this world? Won't you make the most of everything you have and all that you have got?

Life is a transitory experience. We never know which day would be our very last one on this planet. When most people get to that point, they feel as if life just passed them by. They kept waiting for some glorious day when they would do the things they had been postponing forever. As a result, they never got to fully live their life.

If you are making every day the best day of your life, then when your time comes to leave this world, you know that you made the most of the life you had been given.

Use Your Best Things Every Day

Also, many people are so afraid of using their best items that they never get to truly enjoy them. The things that bring pleasure and joy to you are meant to be used on a regular basis. Don't pull out that fancy china only when guests come over.

You are worthy of using your best items every day. Give yourself the best that you can afford. Don't keep waiting for Christmas or special occasions. Life is itself the greatest of all occasions. Being alive is itself a good enough reason to rejoice and celebrate.

Turn Your Home into a Sanctuary for Your Soul

Instead of planning an escape away from home, turn your home into a sanctuary of peace and beauty. Trust me, it's possible to do so on any budget. All you really need is enough creativity and planning.

This way, you will be living your most beautiful life in your very own private sanctuary. You won't need to plan a week or month-long vacation away from home only to come back to a space you don't truly appreciate.

Take out your favorite clothes. Wear an apron while doing chores to protect them from staining.

Even if you do stain them, it's alright! Your favorite clothes are meant to be worn and enjoyed. It is better to wear them out than to allow them to keep hanging in your wardrobe forever without ever truly enjoying them.

Live Like the Queen of Your Kingdom

Think about it like this. If you were a queen, how would you live your life? Won't you be surrounded by the very best of everything? Won't you dress your best every single day of your life? Won't you make an effort to be at your best and finest behavior every day?

Well, if no one has ever said this to you before, then let me be the one. You are the Queen of your world. You deserve the best of everything!

From now on, focus on making every single day a celebration. Wear your best, do your best, be your best, use your best. Treat yourself like royalty. Once you make a habit of doing this, you will be amazed by how satisfied and happy you feel with life.

Other people will also see and treat you differently. After all, other people can only treat you as well as you treat yourself.

Celebrate Life

Raise your bar for yourself and for what your life should be like. A well-lived life isn't about celebrating special occasions. It is all about making a special occasion out of every single day of life.

If you have been practicing the gratitude exercises well, then you must be able to see how there is always so much to be grateful for, so much to be appreciated and celebrated.

Love yourself unconditionally and treat yourself the way you would like your special someone to treat you. Your intimate relationships are anyway a reflection of the relationship you have with yourself.

Hence, focus on amazing an amazing relationship with yourself. Pamper and romance yourself whenever possible. You are worthy of it!

Tasks for This Week:

➤ Get rid of clothes that don't bring joy to your heart. This week, wear your favorite clothes every single day. Now, a lot of you would complain that there's nothing in your wardrobe that you actually like wearing. In that case, it might be a good idea to buy a few new outfits (if you can afford it right now). In case that's not possible for you, wear at least one item every day of the week that you genuinely love. Like, your favorite pair of earrings, the scarf that lights up your eyes, the hairband that you absolutely adore but pretty much never actually wear.

➤ Use your best crockery for all your meals this week.

➤ Think about the ways in which you can make your living space more cozy, inspiring, and beautiful. Perhaps, adding a few fresh flowers in a vase brings great cheer to your desk and your heart! Give yourself a chance to think about all the things you love to surround yourself with but generally save up for special occasions or when you have company over. Do some of those things for yourself because you truly deserve it!

➤ You might want to check out this book for inspiration: *Living a Beautiful Life* by Alexandra Stoddard.

Week 5 - Treat Mealtimes as Sacred

Food is not just what you put into your mouth but also what you allow inside your mind and soul. I want to urge you to be meticulous with all your food choices – whether you are planning your afternoon meal, your next book, or your meditation practice.

Invest in high-quality organic food whenever possible. Health truly is the greatest wealth. Drink pure water and juices. Be sure to stay away from processed food and anything that has artificial colorants added to it.

Eat in a Distraction-Free Environment

Eat only wholesome and fresh food. In Ayurveda, it is mentioned that mealtimes should be treated as sacred because they are offerings to the God that dwells within us. The modern practice of watching TV or listening to the radio while eating is very unhealthy.

You aren't just taking in the food and liquids during your meal, you are also absorbing the energy that is being emitted from the TV program or radio show or whatever else is your chosen source of distraction.

If you are watching something negative, like a crime saga or reality TV fights, then you are assimilating low-frequency vibrations. Even if you are eating high-quality wholesome organic food while watching all this negativity, it won't serve you. The negative energy will neutralize the nutritional benefits of your meal.

Also, in order to fully absorb the nutritional content of the food, we must eat with concentration. Even when we are drinking water, we should be fully focused on the water and how it is hydrating and replenishing our body.

The modern practice of eating meals on the go or at one's desk while working on the computer is also detrimental to health. Eating is as much of a spiritual practice as it is a physical one.

You must treat food with reverence and gratitude. At least for this week, I want you to properly schedule your meal times and eat by focusing entirely on the food that you are consuming.

When you finish eating, don't be in a rush to clear the table. Sit around for a few more minutes and offer gratitude for the delicious and nutritious meal you got to enjoy.

Eat Fresh Wholesome Food

Just for this week, I would also urge you to steer clear of fast food and ready-to-eat meals. Ideally, I would like you to eat a freshly prepared meal every time you are eating. But if that's not possible, at least prepare one fresh meal a day. I am sure you will experience a massive difference in energy levels. It doesn't have to be something elaborate or complicated. Even a simple soup or salad would do.

The only caveat is that there should be no processed ingredient in this meal. Everything should be fresh and wholesome. I want you to observe the entire week how different this simple change makes you feel. Anyone who has ever tried this has benefitted majorly. I am sure this will be life-changing for you as well.

Perhaps at the end of this one week, you would want to continue with this practice for the rest of your life. In eastern philosophy, it is said that we become the food that we eat. That's quite literally the truth! We are indeed what we eat.

Shouldn't you be very careful with what you are putting in your mouth then?

Be Careful with All that You Consume

I would also like you to be careful with the type of conversations you have, the shows you watch, the books you read, etc. Feed your mind and soul only what is uplifting and joyous.

Don't feed yourself anything that makes you feel negative, sad, and/or angry.

Life is too short to be wasted whiling away in negativity. If you can do all this for just one week, you will definitely feel a massive shift in your life. And if you get to enjoy the benefits, why not consider continuing these practices for life!

Tasks for This Week:

➤ Decide your mealtimes and stick to the schedule (at least as much as possible).

➤ Eat with mindfulness and gratitude in a distraction-free environment. Focus entirely on what you are eating or drinking. Switch off the TV, radio, wifi, computer, mobile phone. Let each mealtime be a date with your higher self.

➤ To make mealtimes more enjoyable, be sure to use your favorite crockery as you did in the previous week. You deserve to be treated like royalty!

➤ This entire week, stay away from reading, watching, or discussing anything that makes you feel drained and negative. Focus on consuming uplifting content only.

Week 6 – Build a Strong Morning Ritual

How you start your day determines what the rest of your day would be like. If you constantly keep hitting the snooze button and don't wake up until it is 8.30 or 9.00 am, you are bound to start your day in a rushed manner.

You end up feeling as if life is completely out of your control. You also harbor guilt and shame as you didn't fulfill a promise that you made to yourself about waking up at a specific time in order to accomplish all the goals you have set for the day.

This week, I want you to draft a morning ritual that helps you feel empowered and energized. I would leave it up to you to decide exactly which activities help you in giving a strong start to your day.

The Most Important Time of the Day

The last 30-45 minutes of our day and the 30-45 minute period every morning after we get out of bed are two of the most critical times in the day. You want to be very careful with how you are spending this time because these are the two times in the day when the doors of the subconscious are wide open. Whatever you do then affects you at a deep subconscious level.

I would suggest that you meditate immediately after waking (you can do it after quickly freshening up) and right before going to bed. This way you will get maximum benefits out of your meditation practice.

Incorporate Meditation and Exercise into Your Routine

Pick a meditation practice that resonates with you. The right meditation practice for you would leave you feeling energized and relaxed. You may want to explore different types of practices before finally deciding which one you would like to stick with.

Exercise is another thing you would like to include in your morning ritual. Again, choose a form of exercise that resonates with you. You might enjoy going to the gym more than doing yoga or tai chi. It could also be the other way round. Although it's worth emphasizing here that yoga, tai chi, and qi gong are deeply spiritual practices. Hence, the benefits of these practices go beyond the physical body.

You could also do a mix and match of one or two of these practices. Like you could go to the gym and then do some simple yoga poses to stretch and relax the body later on. Incorporating breathing exercises into the morning routine is another excellent idea as it recharges you at a mental and spiritual level while positively impacting the physical body as well.

Set Clear Intentions and Goals for the Day

Another thing you want to do in the day is set your plan and intentions for the day. Decide three of your top priorities for the day. These should be things that you must accomplish on that day.

At the end of the day, evaluate how successful you had been in achieving your goals.

This will help you remain accountable to yourself. Without setting goals, your day would be aimless. Even if you are just going to relax and take things easy, I would like you to note that down. This way you won't feel guilty about spending your day in a specific way as even your relaxation is intentional.

The whole point is to become more mindful and intentional with your usage of time.

Have a Hearty Breakfast

Another thing you might or might not want to incorporate in your day is a nice hearty breakfast. Some people would love to sit down properly for a good breakfast but are never able to make the time for it. If that sounds like you, then I would suggest that you prioritize having a good breakfast every morning.

To make things easier, you can decide what you want to have for breakfast the previous night itself. I would even suggest that you set the table well in advance. A beautifully set table would further motivate you to properly sit down for breakfast the next morning.

In case, this isn't something you want to do every morning, at least be sure to have something that helps you feel refreshed. It could be something simple like a glass of freshly squeezed citrus juice or a whole fruit that you particularly enjoy eating.

Read Inspiring Quotes

I would also suggest that you write down some of your most favorite quotes that truly inspire you. Read them every morning. Maybe you can also write them down again in your journal that you are using to plan your day. This will give you added motivation to conquer your day.

Take the time to nourish your body (through exercise and healthy food/drinks), mind (by reading something inspiring and setting intentions for & planning the day properly), and soul (through meditation and stillness) every single morning. Don't make excuses by saying that you don't have enough time to do all this.

Start waking up early so that you have enough time to get started with your day on your own terms. You will be significantly more productive and efficient throughout the day.

Tasks for This Week:

➤ Create a custom morning ritual for yourself and commit to it.

➤ Be sure to include activities that nurture you at all three levels – body, mind, and soul.

➤ Try to meditate within the 30-45 minute window upon waking up. Repeat the same in the 30-45 minute window before retiring to bed.

➤ If you enjoy having a hearty breakfast, then set the table and decide the menu the previous night itself. Have your breakfast using your best crockery in a relaxed and distraction-free environment.

➤ I would highly recommend reading *The Miracle Morning* by Hal Elrod if you need more guidance with creating your custom morning routine.

Week 7 – Do Something You Have Been Procrastinating On

Almost all of us suffer from procrastination in one area of life or another. In my experience fear is the root cause of procrastination. Sometimes we are afraid of doing something because we fear it will be very hard or maybe even boring.

Procrastination is a major confidence killer. It leaves us with guilt and hopelessness. On the other hand, when you are able to get yourself to do something you'd rather not do, it gives you a major confidence boost.

Discipline Yourself to Do the Tough Things

Getting in the habit of doing things that you would preferably put off for later (or never) makes you feel better about yourself. This is why I have been laying so much emphasis on starting the day right. For instance, if you are hitting the snooze button to go back to sleep, you don't feel good about yourself when you finally do wake up. Isn't it?

There's a famous saying, *"how you do anything is how you do everything."* No one's quite sure where exactly this adage comes from. Some attribute it to Zen Buddhism. Either way, I really think this is a universal truth.

If you are allowing procrastination to get the better of you in one area of life, it is only a matter of time that you would soon be procrastinating in other areas of life too. Hence, wake up as soon as the alarm goes off every morning.

Make your bed and don't hang out around it until you are ready to retire at night. Making your bed every morning will give you a sense of accomplishment as you have already ticked off one important task. As a result, it will motivate you to achieve more throughout the day.

I hope you are determined to continue following your morning rituals this week as well. If you can make a permanent habit out of it, I can guarantee you that your life would completely transform.

Analyze What You Have Been Procrastinating On

For this week, I would like you to write down everything you have been procrastinating on – big and small. Do some soul-searching to see why exactly you have been procrastinating on these things. Write down what your fear, inhibition, or any other negative feelings around that task are.

Pick up one thing from that list that you are most reluctant to do and just get started with it. Simply getting started is half the battle won.

> *"The journey of a thousand miles begins with one step." – Lao Tzu*

No matter how difficult, overwhelming, or downright scary a task seems, once you get started, it becomes easier.

> *"You don't have to see the whole staircase, just take the first step." – Martin Luther King Jr.*

You might feel like quitting but don't do it. Persistence and perseverance are always rewarded. You don't need to know exactly how you will achieve the goal you have set for yourself. All you need to do is focus on your next step. Eventually, you will achieve your final goals.

Maybe the most important task you have been procrastinating on isn't something that requires a long time to be completed. If it's something you can complete in one or two or three days, then I would urge you to pick another task from the list and complete that as well.

The Secret to Feeling Happy and Fulfilled

You will see for yourself how amazing you feel when you are able to complete tasks that bring out a lot of resistance in you. It's also not important that you have to complete your chosen task or tasks this week itself. Some tasks might take weeks or maybe even years to complete.

What I want you to do this week is to simply get started with these tasks and build a tempo around pursuing them.

The greatest potential for growth usually lies in doing the things that we resist the most.

In doing tasks that seem overwhelming, difficult, or scary, you will grow as a person. As your pain threshold goes to the next level. What was previously very difficult will eventually become easy.

Get Stagnant Energy Moving

Also, at the energetic level when we are procrastinating on something, it begins accumulating stagnant negative energy. By simply getting started, you are getting the stagnant energy moving.

You will definitely feel a shift inside yourself at the energetic and spiritual level. If you can persevere without quitting, you will eventually turn your dreams into reality.

It's okay if you want to take a break once in a while – just don't make a habit out of it. After every break come back with double the amount of force and determination to preserve in your efforts.

In his book, *Eat that Frog*, Brian Tracy suggests tackling the most difficult task of your day in the early half of the day. Schedule the easier tasks for later in the day. I think this is another excellent productivity tip that helps address the problem of procrastinating difficult tasks in our daily lives.

Tasks for This Week:

➤ Schedule some time alone to create an exhaustive list of everything you have been procrastinating on (both big and small).

➤ Pick up one thing that brings out the greatest resistance in you. Analyze to see what kind of feelings this task arouses in you. Do you feel fearful, overwhelmed? What exactly are the feelings that the idea of doing this task evokes in you?

➤ Get started with this task that you have been procrastinating on. If it's something that can be completed in a day or a few days, then consider picking up another such task to complete this week.

➤ Note down how you feel by getting started with/completing the task that you have been procrastinating on? This will help you in acquiring the motivation to complete other tasks you have been procrastinating on. Eventually, you want to make a habit out of this. Every time, you start procrastinating on something, you'll immediately get back to business and start attacking the task that's bringing out so much resistance in you.

Week 8 – Do Something Loving and Kind

We had covered this in the first book. It is again one of those basics we need to master for a happy life. Hence, we would discuss this idea in more depth now.

The only way to be truly happy in life is to focus on giving rather than on receiving. You might think that giving implies something being taken away from you. It is actually the opposite.

Whatever you give to others comes back to you manifold. A poor person is one who focuses only on receiving and doesn't care about giving.

"You have not lived a perfect day unless you've done something for someone who will never be able to repay you."— Ruth Smeltzer

Give From Your Heart

I can guarantee you that giving will enrich your life in more ways than you can imagine. The only catch is that you have to give from a place of selflessness and unconditional love.

Every time I want to give something to someone, I always ask myself, "Would I want to give to this person even if I was going to receive nothing in return – not even an acknowledgment or appreciation?"

If the answer is 'yes,' then I know that I have the right motivations behind that desire to give. If the answer is 'no,' then maybe giving is not the best thing in that situation. It will likely evoke frustration, resentment, and disappointment in me.

My formula is simple: give from the heart or don't give at all. I feel this is an essential life skill to master if you want to be happy.

Become Self-Sufficient

To master this attitude, we have to first become self-sufficient. If we need love, appreciation, or even acknowledgment from others, then we aren't really free. Other people have power over us and can determine whether we are living a happy or an unhappy life.

Hence, mastering self-love and self-nourishment is essential for becoming a giving person. You have to give to yourself everything that you desire to receive from another. Like, if you want someone to appreciate you, then first you will have to learn to appreciate yourself. You can't expect someone else to give you appreciation when you are constantly criticizing yourself.

As we discussed earlier, the relationships we have with others is a direct reflection of the relationship we have with ourselves. People can treat us only as well as we treat ourselves. The interesting thing is that when we treat ourselves with self-respect and dignity, we won't put up with negative treatment by another.

So first you have to fill your cup. That's what we focused on in all the precious weeks and we will continue to work on it in the upcoming weeks as well. This week, I want you to focus on giving to others alongside everything else that you are doing for your own self.

Giving Can be Both Big and Small

The problem with the idea of 'giving' is that most people immediately start thinking they have to do something grand and massive. That's not how it works. Giving happens on many different levels. Giving a compliment to a stranger is as much of an act of love and kindness as is donating a large sum of money to a charity.

In fact, every person in this world is hungry for love and appreciation. If you can offer it to someone, it will touch them in more ways than you can imagine.

"The hunger for love is much more difficult to remove than the hunger for bread." – Mother Teresa

Give love, appreciation, kindness, and your undivided attention to others. If you have a selfless heartfelt desire to help someone monetarily, then do that as well.

Give to others what you wish to receive for yourself. I can guarantee you that whatever you are giving will eventually come back to you multiplied.

However, the catch is that you can't make that a motivation for giving to others. Giving should always be done from a place of complete selflessness and unconditional love. The very act of giving should be its own reward.

Task for This Week:

➤ This week, do something loving and kind for someone. It doesn't have to be something grand. Even a sincere compliment given to another person qualifies as an act of love and kindness.

➤ Note down how you felt when you gave something to someone from a place of selflessness and unconditional love.

➤ If you really enjoyed giving, then consider doing something loving and kind for another person every day from now on. (You don't have to get stressed about it – just be on the lookout for opportunities to serve others). You will be amazed by how much more beautiful your life becomes if you can make a habit out of this!

Week 9 – Pursue a Hobby

A hobby is something that brings great joy to the heart.

We live in a society that is obsessed with productivity and the commercial value of everything. Most of us have forgotten the simple pleasure of doing something for the sake of the joy that it brings to our hearts.

"No man is really happy or safe without a hobby." – William Osler

Find Your Favorite Hobby

This week, I want you to think about something that you absolutely love doing. It shouldn't be something you are trying to turn into a commercial product but anything that you simply enjoy doing solely for the pleasure it gives you. Maybe it's calligraphy, painting, flower-making, baking, or anything else that appeals to you.

I wouldn't include reading on this list as I consider daily reading to be an essential practice for personal development and self-care.

By thinking about your hobbies this week, you might get reminded of the things you used to truly enjoy doing but haven't done in a very long time simply because you couldn't find the time for them.

"A hobby a day keeps the doldrums away." –
Phyllis McGinley

Pursuing Your Hobby is Always Worthwhile

Don't think of pursuing your hobby as a waste of productive time. Time that is spent intentionally is never wasted. Pursuing your favorite hobby will help you feel relaxed and happy. This in turn will make you more efficient and productive at work.

I am not saying that you spend every single day of this week pursuing your hobby, but at least give it one day or maybe just one hour in the entire week. Observe how it makes you feel. Most likely, you'll feel amazing and would want to do it again.

Ideally, you would want to work on your hobby at least once a week. Pursuing your favorite hobby is nothing short of meditation. The joy that it brings to your heart helps in getting you to be fully present in the here and now.

You might even get some brilliant ideas while doing your hobby since your mind is in a relaxed space where it isn't thinking about moving towards a particular goal.

Hobbies Help Up Connect with Like-Minded People

Hobbies are also great for connecting with other like-minded people. It is a commonly-known fact in the business community that more deals are struck on the golf course than they are in a boardroom.

Even if you aren't an entrepreneur or a business person, pursuing your hobbies can be an excellent way of networking with others.

Besides, isn't it thrilling and exciting when you get to discuss with someone a topic of genuine interest to you and that person shares your excitement!

If you want to pursue your hobby in isolation, that's fine too.

You are doing an act of love and kindness to yourself by pursuing your hobby. You're gifting yourself a chance to do something that brings you great joy.

Set Up a Hobby Corner for Yourself

I would highly recommend that you create a hobby corner for yourself (if possible). This would be a space where all the tools and paraphernalia related to your hobby are housed.

Hence, you won't be wasting time looking for them and setting up your workstation every time you want to work on your hobby.

This could mean different things for different people. For instance, if your hobby is golf, then you can create a dedicated corner for housing all your golf-gear. You could also get yourself a membership to the country club and schedule a time in your calendar for the day on which you would be playing golf.

If your hobby is painting, your hobby corner could be a space where all your canvases, easels, and painting equipment are housed. As soon as you find the time to spend on your hobby, you can switch gears by entering this space. Since everything is already set up, your mind won't get the time to talk you out of it. You can also schedule time in your calendar for when you would be painting.

These are just two examples of how you can bring about a greater level of commitment to the pursuit of your hobbies. It will definitely be a rewarding experience for you.

If you have a lot of hobbies and you have a spare room, then maybe you can also create a hobby room for yourself. This would be a dedicated space where you go for enjoying all your hobbies.

Tasks for This Week:

➤ Make a list of your favorite hobbies.

➤ Spend at least one hour this week pursuing your favorite hobby. If you want, you can also choose to do it every day of the week for one hour or so. However, that's not essential. If you can only spend one hour on your hobby this entire week, that works well too.

➤ Note down in your journal how you felt after spending time on your hobby. Consider turning hobby-time into a regular habit.

Week 10 – Read for at Least 10 Minutes Daily

If you read about the lives of the most successful people, you will recognize one common theme. Almost all of them are voracious readers.

"Not all readers are leaders, but all leaders are readers." Harry Truman

Reading is an act of great self-care. It helps you learn from the wisdom and experiences of others even if you might not have experienced the same circumstances in your own reality.

This gives you the ability to avoid making the same mistakes as someone else might have made while you still get to incorporate into your life the wisdom that they gained through it.

Find Your Niche

If you want to be successful in life (whatever your definition and idea of success is), you must read regularly. This week I would like you to create a list of all the subjects that interest you. Then I would like you to decide which subject will help you level up your life almost immediately.

For instance, two subjects you are interested in could be art history and health. Studying art history will give you a deeper appreciation of art but learning about health will help you get fitter.

Hence, in this case, you should prioritize reading about health. On the other hand, maybe your immediate goal is to get a college degree in art history, then, prioritizing art history would serve you better.

Picking the right subject to focus on depends entirely upon your individual interests, circumstances, and goals. If you can't figure out which subject to prioritize, then I would recommend going to the self-help section of any bookstore (or online) and picking a book that appeals most to you.

At the end of this chapter, I have included a list of general self-help books that you can consider checking out.

Ready Daily for at Least 10 Minutes

Once you have found a book that interests you, commit to reading it every single day for at least 10 minutes. That's not a lot to ask for. Anyone can take that much time out of the day for reading.

You can also think out of the box to figure out how you can incorporate reading into your daily life. Maybe, the perfect reading time for you is when you are taking the train back home in the evening or you could listen to an audiobook while doing daily chores.

Commit at least 10 minutes every day to learning and bettering your mind (separate from the time you spend reading this book).

Do you realize what this means in a week? It means you would have clocked in 70 minutes of reading-time within a week! I think that's amazing!!

Internalize the Wisdom

Also, when you are reading, don't do it mindlessly or as just another task you want to get done with. Ponder over what you are reading; think about the ways in which you can incorporate that information into your life.

I read somewhere that the best way to learn is by turning the information you have acquired into a practical experience for yourself. So think of ways in which you can take action on what you are learning.

Here's a suggested reading list in case you aren't sure where to get started. Pick up any book that truly appeals to you and focus on reading it daily until you finish it or you feel like you have gained all the wisdom out of it as was possible for you:

- *You Can Heal Your Life* by Louise L. Hay

- *How to Win Friends & Influence People* by Dale Carnegie

- *The 7 Habits of Highly Effective People* by Stephen. R. Covey

- *Eat That Frog!* by Brian Tracy

- *Think and Grow Rich* by Napoleon Hill

- *The Power of Now* by Eckhart Tolle

- *Rich Dad Poor Dad* by Robert Kiyosaki

- *The Richest Man in Babylon* by George Samuel Clason

- *The Power of Positive Thinking* by Norman Vincent Peale

- *The Seven Spiritual Laws of Success: A Practical Guide to the Fulfillment of Your Dreams* by Deepak Chopra

- *Ask and it is Given: Learning to Manifest Your Desires* by Esther and Jerry Hicks

Tasks for This Week:

➤ Note down the genres and subjects of your interest. I would suggest listing those subjects and genres that will endow you with the desired skills to improve your life.

➤ Take the time to decide learning about which subject will help you bring about a significant improvement in your life.

➤ Read for at least 10 minutes daily.

➤ Ponder over the information you have acquired. If it is something actionable, then write down how you will be acting on it in a practical manner. If it's not something actionable, then think about your own stance on what the author has to say. Do you agree or disagree with the author? Maybe your stance is more complex somewhere in the middle. The whole point of learning is to internalize the information you are exposing yourself to. This can happen only through critical thinking and/or practical experience.

Week 11 – Write a Love Letter to Yourself

Self-care is all about self-love. As we have discussed previously in this book and in book one, it's not about narcissism.

True self-love makes us indestructible because we are no longer dependent upon others for the fulfillment of our needs.

As a result, we become even more deeply appreciative of the love and affection that does come from others. That's because now we aren't really expecting it – it becomes a special gift that we get to cherish and enjoy whenever it is voluntarily offered.

Why and How to Write a Love Letter to Yourself

This week I want you to write a love letter to yourself. Now, I know that many of you would squirm at this idea. You might have been conditioned to believe that doing anything like this would be purely narcissistic.

I can assure you that this would be a deeply healing experience for you.

You will likely experience a lot of emotions as you write the letter to yourself and when you take the time to read it.

No matter how strong the resistance is, I want to urge you to give this a try. You will definitely gain something out of this.

Before you sit down to write the letter, I would like you to create a list of all the things that you wish other people said to you. Look deep into your soul to find that which your heart truly aches to hear.

When you finally sit down to write that letter, address it to yourself as if you really are another person who would be reading it.

Tell yourself how amazing, gorgeous, and intelligent you are. Apologize for anything negative you might have said to yourself and that from now on, you will only offer words of encouragement to yourself.

It Will be a Worthwhile Experience for You

I'm not saying that this is going to be an easy exercise for you. You will most likely experience a lot of limiting beliefs as you pen down this letter. Your ego might even say things like, "Who do you think you are," "You really believe that about yourself," "What makes you think you deserve all this!"

No matter what your ego says, continue writing the letter showering yourself with the praise and appreciation that your heart deeply longs to hear.

Why Praise is a Better Motivator than Criticism

Most people think that the only way to get themselves or others to improve is through criticism. This is a terrible misconception. Criticism often destroys the human spirit.

Think of it like this, there's this little baby who is just learning to walk. He falls down every time after taking a few steps. Now, if you start hurling abuses at the baby, telling him he's never going to learn how to walk properly; he's good for nothing; etc., what do you think it would do to the baby?

Obviously, you would never do that to a baby, isn't it? You will cheer on the baby however few steps he is able to take. Praise and appreciation are often better motivators than criticism.

Every time, you get yourself to do something good, appreciate your efforts instead of criticizing everything you aren't able to do right. This positive feedback will give you the motivation to further improve and do better next time.

For instance, if you managed to stick to a healthy diet for four days in the week but experienced a little bit of weakness on the fifth day (or maybe you totally lost control on that one day), appreciate yourself for the five days when you did stick with the diet instead of beating yourself up for the one day when you couldn't.

Discipline yourself but do it with positive feedback and constructive criticism. Like, if you couldn't get the results you desired, then, ask yourself what you can do better next time and resolve to do things differently when the opportunity arises again.

This is a much better and far more practical approach than calling yourself names or saying things like, "You can never do anything right," "You always mess everything up, "You're so stupid and dumb."

Often these are words that we hear from others while growing up. Unfortunately, they became deeply embedded into our psyche as we adopted the voice of the authority figures from our childhood who themselves knew nothing better. They thought they were helping us; not realizing how damaging their words and actions really were.

Love can heal all wounds and the person whose love you need the most is you yourself. Hence, you must write this letter to yourself. You deserve it!

Tasks for This Week:

➤ Make a list of all the things you have ever wished to hear from others.

➤ Write a love letter to yourself saying all the things that you wish you had heard from others. Be sure to tell yourself how amazing, gorgeous, intelligent, and smart you are.

➤ Read this letter whenever you need a little encouragement and appreciation. Later on, you might want to add many other things (feel free to modify the letter whenever you feel like). Maybe you would even want to write another letter to yourself at a later date.

I would also encourage you to consider making a habit out of this. The letter doesn't have to be long but it should always be heartfelt. Perhaps you could write a few lines to yourself every day, every week, every month, or maybe even every year. Do what feels best to you as this is all about getting yourself to feel loved and appreciated.

Week 12 – Find a Reason for Celebration

Why wait for a special occasion when you can create one?

Every week find a reason to celebrate life. One great idea would be to look at the map and find a country that interests you. Read a bit about their special occasions, and then figure out how you can replicate a similar celebration in your own home. You can create a calendar of holidays based on special occasions celebrated in different countries across the world.

This practice would be especially fun if you have kids. It is both an educational and a celebratory experience.

If you think this is a bit too preposterous, then you can find something else to celebrate every week. It could be something as trivial as celebrating the fact that you woke up early every day of the week or something really big like a major hike in income.

No reason is too trivial for celebration. Life is itself the greatest of all gifts.

Get Together with Your Loved Ones Every Week

Find a reason to bring your loved ones together at least once a week. If you have nothing else to celebrate, then you can simply celebrate the fact that you have each other to love and support.

Don't take anything for granted ever. Celebrate every blessing that you have in your life.

Make it a Glamorous Affair

Ask everyone to wear their finest party wear clothes. You will enjoy life so much more when you give yourself a reason to wear your most glamorous clothes every week. It will also motivate you to exercise regularly and eat healthy as you would want to look your best at your weekly celebrations.

I hope that by now you have embraced the mindset of looking, feeling, and being your best on a daily basis.

Having a weekly celebration will also deepen the bond that you and your loved ones share. Just be sure to spend your shared time together talking about positive and uplifting things. Steer clear of gossip and negativity.

I must emphasize that I am not suggesting you get together regularly with family members who have a less than positive impact on your life and psyche. I'm talking about getting together with those loved ones whose company you truly enjoy but due to the busyness of life, you end up not spending enough time with them.

Write Letters to Each Other

You can also exchange letters at these gatherings. For instance, people can be paired together. Each person would write a letter of gratitude and appreciation for the other. If you end up with an odd number, then maybe as the host of the party, you can offer to exchange an additional letter with that person.

These are just some ideas to get you started – use your creativity and imagination to come up with what works best for you.

Don't be Afraid to Celebrate Alone

In case you live far away from your loved ones, you can consider doing a weekly celebration all by yourself. You can wear your best evening dress and go to a place you really love or you can order a delivery or maybe you can cook your favorite meal.

You can spend the evening relaxing and doing the things that you love. The point is to have a weekly celebration – how you do it or who you do it with is up to you.

Tasks for This Week:

➤ Find a reason to have a celebration this week.

➤ Invite your loved ones over (highly recommended) or celebrate the occasion by yourself.

➤ Try to get in the habit of having a weekly celebration from now on. Don't stress yourself out over it though. Follow your heart and do what feels uplifting and good to you! You're doing this to increase your happiness and satisfaction. It's not meant to create additional stress in your life.

If the idea of having a weekly celebration stresses you out, then don't do it. You can still do something special for yourself every week – something that leaves you feeling happy and relaxed.

Bonus Chapter – Random Self-Care Ideas for You to Try Out

➤ Buy yourself fresh flowers for no reason.

➤ Spend the evening reading your favorite book.

➤ Take some time off to simply relax and dream.

➤ Write a 'thank you' note to someone.

➤ Have a warm cup of hot cocoa on a cold day.

➤ Illuminate your room with beautiful lamps.

➤ Have a candlelit bath.

➤ Prepare your favorite meal.

➤ Buy yourself a special gift.

➤ Call someone you love for no reason.

➤ Say 'I love you' to someone who means the world to you.

➤ Organize your work desk in a way that gives you joy.

➤ Wake up early to watch the sunrise.

➤ Go for a walk in nature.

➤ Take some time out for bird-watching.

➤ Take the time to marvel at the beauty of a butterfly.

➤ Go to a place where you can see the night sky without any light pollution.

➤ Play scrabble or your favorite board game with your special someone.

➤ Illuminate your room with beautiful lamps.

➤ Bake a special dish and present it to someone who would appreciate it.

➤ Have a picnic in the garden or park.

➤ Illuminate your room with beautiful lamps.

➤ Start a herb garden on your window sill.

➤ Kickstart your day with a glass of freshly squeezed citrus juice every morning.

➤ Drink chamomile tea before bed.

➤ Organize a barbecue for family and friends.

➤ Play with small children.

➤ Listen to soothing and calming music.

➤ Go hiking somewhere beautiful.

➤ Just relax – do nothing.

➤ Book a spa day for yourself.

➤ Get your hair and makeup done by a professional.

➤ Watch the sunset over a lake or any other water body.

➤ Enjoy a decadent bowl of hot soup on a cold evening.

➤ Take time out to smell the roses.

➤ Walk bare feet in the grass.

➤ Turn the lights off and spend the entire evening in candlelight

➤ Wear cashmere socks in winter.

➤ In summer, wear the finest quality linen and cotton you can afford

➤ Give yourself the luxury of wearing silk whenever possible. If all you can afford is a silk headband, then go for it!

➤ Sleep on a silk pillowcase to protect your hair and skin (totally worth investing in).

I Need Your Help...

I want to thank you for taking this 12-week journey with me. I hope that I have been able to help you with transforming your life and your relationship with yourself.

Even though this book has come to an end, please understand that this is only the beginning of a new life for you. I want to urge you to continue the self-love and self-care practices you have adopted through this book.

No matter what you are going through in life, please never forget that you can't pour from an empty cup. Prioritize your needs above everything else because you can give to others when you have more than enough for yourself.

If this book has proven helpful to you in any way, then I'd like to ask you for a favor. Would you be kind enough to write a review for this book on Amazon?

It's my dream to help as many people as possible through my work. Your testimony might inspire someone else to pick this book and change their life. So please, do leave a review.

Thank you for taking this Course in Self-Care with me!

Book 1 of the series

A COURSE IN

Self-Care

HEAL YOUR BODY, MIND & SOUL THROUGH SELF-LOVE AND MINDFULNESS

ANKITA S.

A Course in Self-Care 3 & 4 _Coming Soon!_

Printed in Great Britain
by Amazon